The Stranger

by Albert Camus

A Study Guide by Ray Moore

Portrait of Albert Camus, 1957.

Copyright:

Ray Moore 2016

Where I have selectively quoted from the writings of others in the course of my own argument, I have done so in the sincere belief that this constitutes fair use.

Contents

Preface 1
Introduction 2
Dramatis Personæ – List of Characters in Order of Appearance 4
Genre 7
Narrative Voice 7
Themes 9
The Stranger A Study Guide: 13
    Part One 15
    Part Two 22
Glossary 31
    Appendix 1: A Structure for Understanding The Stranger Part 2, Chapter 5 ... 32
    Appendix 2: The Trial of Meursault 34
    Appendix 3: Graphic organizers 37
        #1: Plot 37
        #2: Different perspectives on the situation which initiates the action in the novel 38
    Appendix 4: Classroom Use of the Study Guide Questions 39
    Appendix 5: Guide to Further Reading 41
    Appendix 6: Bibliography 44
To the Reader 47

The Stranger by Albert Camus

Preface

At the outset, I should make clear that the text of the sections entitled Genre, Narrative Voice and Themes is taken (with significant revision) from my book *"The Stranger" by Albert Camus: A Critical Introduction* (Revised Edition). The Directed Study Questions and Commentary also appear in that book.

I admit to being an unashamed 'absurdist' (the meaning of the term will become clear as you read on). I have learned more about the meaninglessness of life – or rather, the meaning that humans can give to their lives – from Camus than from any other writer. My aim in this book is to share my enthusiasm for Camus' ideas by making them more easily accessible to the reader.

There is a danger that, by placing the introductory materials *before* the Study Questions, the reader's approach to *The Stranger* itself may be prejudiced. The reader who is approaching Camus' text for the first time might, therefore, prefer to skip straight to the Study Guide and use the questions as an aid to reading the text, coming back to the materials in the earlier sections only after having done so.

Illustration:

The portrait of Albert Camus is from New York World-Telegram and the Sun Newspaper Photograph Collection, 1957. (Source: Wikipedia. It is part of a collection donated to the Library of Congress. There are no known restrictions on the usage of this photograph.)

Introduction

Plot Summary:

The story is set in French Algeria in the years immediately before the Second World War. Meursault (only his surname is ever given) is a shipping clerk in Algiers. He is in his early twenties and (presumably) quite handsome. Since he placed his aging mother in an old people's in Marengo, he has lived quietly in the apartment that they once shared. Asocial rather than anti-social, Meursault seems to go through life as an uncommitted observer. All of this changes, however, when a telegram from the Director of the home informs him of the death of his mother.

In quick succession, Meursault is involved in: traveling to attend his mother's funeral, a passionate affair with the beautiful Marie, an offer of promotion that involves moving to Paris, the problems of one of his neighbors and the man's sick dog, and finally the plans of a local pimp to beat up one of his working girls. The girl is an Arab, and the beating that the pimp gives her leads to a confrontation on the beach with her brother and his friends which ultimately leads to Meursault shooting the brother.

Meursault is put on trial, but as the trial develops he seems to be accused not simply of killing a man but of living his entire life without belief in either the religious or civic values that hold society together. Condemned as a monster who effectively killed his mother, Meursault is sentenced to be executed. Shortly before the sentence is carried out, however, he comes to understand the true relationship between man and a meaningless universe.

Why Read this Book?

There is no doubt that *The Stranger* is one of the greatest novels of the twentieth century and that it will continue to be read in the twenty-first century. In terms of style, it is also an easy book to read, but one that leaves the reader with a lot to think about.

The popularity of *The Stranger* rests on the fact that since its publication it has continued to capture its readers' sense of being alienated from those forces in society that seek to impose order, morality, and conformity. Patrick McCarthy writes that "*The Stranger's* importance ... lies in the way that the novel has caught fundamental traits of modern individualism: the determination to trust one's own experience while distrusting the many and varied forms of authority" (103). This is one of the reasons why many teenage readers instinctively empathize with (or 'get') Meursault.

The Stranger by Albert Camus

Important: Issues with this Book:

There are no graphic descriptions of sex or violence or suffering. There is no bad language.

A Note on the graphic organizers

Two graphic organizers are provided to enable the students to make notes. Some simple guidance will be needed depending on how the teacher wants them to be used.

A Study Guide

Dramatis Personæ – List of Characters in Order of Appearance

Madame Meursault – Three years before the beginning of the narrative, Meursault sent his elderly mother to a home in the village of Marengo. Always silent, Madame Meursault seemed simply to watch her son who found their failure to communicate increasingly difficult to live with. When she dies, Meursault feels obligated to attend her funeral, but he sheds no tears for her passing and seems impatient at the funeral rituals that appears so important to others connected with his mother. However, as the narrative progresses, Meursault increasingly comes to understand and to identify with his mother believing that, toward the end of her life, she too must have understood and embraced the meaninglessness of the universe and lived by her own 'rules,' and values, just as he eventually does.

Meursault – The protagonist and narrator of *The Stranger* is a shipping clerk in Algiers, the capital of colonial French Algeria. Since moving his mother into the old people's home, Meursault has lived alone in an apartment that is rather too big for a single person. He is a detached figure who observes rather than participates in the life of Algiers. The death of his mother begins a process which disturbs Meursault's passivity and isolation and leads eventually to a confrontation with an Arab on a beach outside the town. Meursault kills the man, shooting him five times. As a result, he is put on trial. However, as the trial proceeds it becomes clear that society is judging and condemning Meursault for his indifference to the civil and religious values which hold society together. As such, he is an alien, a monster, who represents a serious challenge to the society in which he lives.

Céleste – The proprietor of the small neighborhood café where Meursault habitually eats lunch, Céleste is never put off by his quiet and withdrawn personality. At Meursault's trial, he testifies that Meursault is an honest, decent man, who had the bad luck to shoot an Arab.

The Caretaker – The caretaker at the Marengo home where Meursault's mother lived offers to open the casket for Meursault to view his mother's body. The two get on quite well; they drink coffee and smoke together during the vigil, which will be used against Meursault at his trial.

The Director – The manager of the Marengo home assures Meursault that he should not feel guilty for having sent his mother to live there and that she was perfectly happy. During Meursault's trial, however, his testimony that Meursault did not show the normal signs of a grieving son is used against Meursault.

Thomas Pérez – In the months before her death, Madame Meursault and Pérez

The Stranger by Albert Camus

had become so close that the other residents joked that he was her fiancé. Pérez genuinely mourns her death and makes valiant (but essentially comic and futile) attempts to keep up with her cortege on its way to the burial. His testimony will also be used against Meursault at his trial.

Marie Cardona – Meursault meets Marie, a beautiful former co-worker, quite my chance, the day after his mother's funeral and begins a passionate affair with her. Meursault enjoys being with Marie, but when Marie suggests that they should marry he tells her that, though they can be married if she wants to, he does not love her. After his arrest, Marie tries to support him by making the one visit to the prison where he is held that she is allowed and by attending the trial.

Emmanuel – He is a co-worker with whom Meursault often had lunch.

Salamano – A neighbor and acquaintance of Meursault, Salamano is an old widower whose only companion is an old dog that suffers from mange. Salamano frequently curses and beats the dog, but when it runs away he is devastated by the loss.

Raymond Sintès – A local pimp who lives in the same apartment block as Meursault, Sintès enlists Meursault's help in luring his 'mistress' (actually a young woman he has been running as a prostitute) to a meeting so that he can punish her for being unfaithful. The beating Sintès administers is quite brutal, bringing him (and by association Meursault) into conflict with both the police and with the girl's brother. This leads directly to the confrontation on the beach where Meursault kills the Arab. Ironically, Sintès avoids prosecution for anything.

Masson – One of Sintès' friends, Masson invites Sintès, Meursault, and Marie to spend a Sunday at his beach house just outside Algiers with him and his wife. It is while walking on the beach with Sintès and Meursault that the first of two violent encounters with the Arabs occurs.

The Arab – The brother of Sintès' 'mistress' obviously determines to get revenge on Sintès who notices the man and his friends keeping the apartment building under observation. On the Sunday when Sintès, Meursault, and Marie take a bus to Masson's beach house, the Arabs follow them and there is a violent confrontation on the beach. (One of the most common criticisms of the novel is that the Arab remains anonymous being given neither a name nor an identity.)

The Examining Magistrate – The magistrate is in charge of the investigation of the shooting of the Arab by Meursault. A deeply (or at least a conventionally) religious man, he is disturbed by Meursault's apparent lack of grief over his crime. In an effort to make him confess and call on God for divine mercy, the magistrate brandishes a crucifix in front of Meursault's face and demands that he show belief in God's mercy. When Meursault firmly asserts his lack of belief, the magistrate dismisses him as "Monsieur Antichrist."

The Prosecutor – At the trial, the prosecutor presents Meursault as lacking humanity and moral values. He presents the shooting of the Arab as merely the consequence of Meursault's moral indifference of which he cites his lack of emotional attachment to his mother as the most important manifestation. He demands the death penalty for Meursault because his amorality threatens all of society.

The Chaplain – After Meursault is found guilty and sentenced to death, he repeatedly refuses to see the chaplain, but, as the execution draws near, the chaplain visits Meursault's cell anyway. Like the magistrate, the chaplain's fragile faith is threatened by Meursault's certainty that the universe is entirely without meaning. Angrily, Meursault rejects the chaplain's pleas that he must find hope in the mercy of God. Their argument triggers Meursault's final epiphany: he comes to understand that the meaninglessness of the universe does not mean (as he had always supposed) that life is entirely arbitrary and without value.

Genre

The novel is a *bildungsroman*, that is, a narrative that centers on the moral and intellectual growth of the young protagonist. Understanding this point will prevent a great deal of misunderstanding. English Showalter Jr. states that "*The Stranger* relates *a progress toward understanding*" (93 emphasis added). The news of his mother's death begins a sequence of events which will pull Meursault out of his comfortable cocoon of disengagement until he is face to face with life's ultimate question. Meursault only comes fully to understand man's relationship with the world and with his own mortality (the two are essentially the same thing) at the end of the novel.

Narrative Voice

The central paradox of the text is that the protagonist/narrator is presented in ways that make the reader feel sympathetic to him despite the fact that he facilitates the vicious beating of a young Arab woman whom he does not know and shoots an Arab man who poses no actual threat to him. Any understanding of the novel must address this apparent contradiction.

Meursault's story is told in the first-person, a technique which disposes the reader to empathize with the narrator. Two questions must, however, be asked of *any* first person narrative. Firstly: Does the reader *trust* that the narrator gives an accurate account of what happens and a reliable interpretation and evaluation of its significance? Secondly: Is it clear that the author *intends* the reader to trust the narrator? Everything is fine provided that the answers to these questions are either *both* in the affirmative or *both* in the negative because each of these implies that the text has consistency and artistic integrity. Problems occur when one of the answers is affirmative and the other negative because this implies a loss of artistic control by the author and a flawed work of art.

Put simply: Meursault is telling us the story, or rather, Meursault is telling the story to himself and we, who are given no identity or independent reality, eavesdrop on his thoughts. Thus, the novel is an interior rather than a dramatic monologue, "a silent meditation addressed to no one" (Showalter 67). This interpretation explains why there is only an *apparent* contradiction between Meursault, the unreflective character in Part One, and Meursault the reflective narrator. Although Meursault does not begin his story until after he has understood its full significance, he makes every effort in the narrative not to interpret past actions on the basis of this future knowledge. Camus ensures that Meursault explains every incident in terms of what he felt and understood *at the time* precisely because what he felt and understood at the time was so often entirely wrong (as he only later comes to understand). To the author, this limited perspective is essential to the aim that the reader should grow to understanding *with* Meursault and not just have Meursault's growth explained *by* an enlightened narrator.

Only very occasionally does Meursault interpose a judgment which depends upon his later knowledge, and on those few occasions when Meursault wishes to draw attention to the difference between how he felt at the time and how he feels now, he makes it perfectly clear that this is what he is doing. As readers, we see everything through Meursault's eyes, which means that initially our familiar world appears rather strange and unfamiliar. Progressively, however, we come to understand and to accept Meursault's perspective so that "we see the world increasingly as arbitrary, capricious, pretentious, even hypocritical" (Sprintzen 24). This means that by the time the spokespeople for society get to make their case against Meursault in Part Two, we are disposed, if not entirely to sympathize with him, at least to judge their viewpoint critically. This is Camus' intention.

The Stranger by Albert Camus

Themes

Man and the Natural World

Human life is measured in decades, but we live out our span on a planet which, though not eternal, has an existence measured in billions of years – 4.54 billion to be precise. Thus, simply to be alive is to be aware of one's mortality: to open oneself to the beauty of the world is to be aware that such beauty existed before we were born and that it will exist, more or less indefinitely, after we are dead. The more acutely we appreciate the beauties of the world, the more melancholy we *must* be about the very short span we have in which to appreciate it.

Taking this perception as a given in his early writings, Albert Camus considers a further precise and limited question: What is the nature of the relationship between man and this world in which he lives out his life? This might seem to be a dauntingly difficult question until we realize that there are fundamentally only three possible answers. The world may be either: benevolent, malevolent, or indifferent – there are no other answers.

The first two viewpoints hold either that humans are fundamentally at home in the natural world or that the two are fundamentally in conflict, both of which are positions that Meursault appears to accept at different points in the novel *The Stranger*. Adherents of the third position, however, hold that the natural world and the universe beyond are alike *indifferent* to man and to human destiny. Unlike the first two viewpoints which imply religious (or at least a spiritual) belief, the third is essentially humanistic, rejecting equally both cosmic karma and divine providence. This represents Meursault's final understanding of man's relationship with the world in which he lives, an understanding which Camus appears to endorse.

The Death of God

> The age of enlightenment has destroyed faith in personal survival; the scars of this operation have never healed. There is a vacancy in every living soul, a deep thirst in all of us. (Arthur Koestler "End of an Illusion")

In 1654, James Ussher, Archbishop of Armagh and Primate of All Ireland, precisely dated Creation to the night preceding Sunday, October 23rd, 4004 BC. In 1794, Archbishop William Paley (1743–1805) published *View of the Evidences of Christianity*, in which he expressed his confidence that "the truths or religion are akin to scientific truths and defensible by the same methods" and that Church dogmas could be supported with "the quiet efficiency of a mathematical demonstration" (quoted in Stone, Wilfred. *The Cave and the Mountain: A Study of E. M. Forster*. 49).

In the nineteenth century, such certainties were rapidly eroded by advances in biology, geology, paleontology, and archeology that cut away the very foundations of historical Christianity. As Martin Booth writes in his biography of Sir Arthur Conan Doyle, "The reason and appeal of Darwin's theories, which he had propounded in his *Origin of Species*, published [in 1859] ..., and in *The Descent of Man*, published in 1871, were such that thinking men found they had no alternative but to accept the premises of science and reject religious belief" (59)

If, as Nietzsche asserts in *The Gay Science* (1882), "God is dead," then the values associated with God are merely human constructs. The Ten Commandments, for example, are no more than graffiti on stone, an idea which, depending on one's point of view, might be regarded either as blasphemous or as liberating. Thus, in 1920, F. Scott Fitzgerald concluded his novel *This Side of Paradise* by describing the protagonist, Amory Blaine, as part of "a new generation ... grown up to find all Gods dead, all wars fought, all faiths in man shaken." *The Stranger* is set firmly in this post-Judeo-Christian world in which transcendent, eternal values have been shown not only to have no validity but to have been a childish delusion precisely because God has ceased to be believable.

If there is no God, then the trappings of religious observance are meaningless; at best they are self-delusion, and at worst a mechanism of social manipulation, coercion and control. More fundamentally, if we are living a life without values and without value, then nihilism appears to be the only intellectually honest response. Western thought had come a long way from the mathematical certainties of Bishop Ussher! This is the intellectual world in which Albert Camus, born into a nominally Catholic family, grew to maturity. Facing the same world as Fitzgerald's Amory Blaine, Camus was deeply concerned that he was living at a time when the ebbing of the tide of faith was leaving a moral and spiritual vacuum. If irrational faith was, to Camus, never a viable option, nihilism was equally unacceptable.

Absurdism

To recap, our understanding of what Camus means by the absurd needs to begin with some fundamental questions: Does life have meaning? If life does not have meaning, why doesn't it? If life is meaningless, what alternative is there to despair? What possible moral objection can there be to suicide?

Any explanation of the concept of a meaningful life will normally include words like "religion," "belief," "faith," "God," and "Divine Providence." Obviously, if there is an eternal God then some entity is in control of the universe, has a plan, knows what it all means, etc. The fact that we mortals might not be able to *see* God's plan does not prove it is not there: our leap of faith, going beyond reason, provides a conviction of transcendent values.

The Stranger by Albert Camus

The conviction that life does not have meaning generally rests on the assumptions that birth is entirely random, and that death is both certain and completely final. The absurd is defined by Camus as the mismatch in an individual's consciousness between the *assumptions* upon which he has been living his life and the *reality* of that life. Thus, the absurd rests neither in the world (which is irrational and random) nor in man (who has an inherent need to find meaning), but rather in the *confrontation* or *interface* between the "unreasonable silence of the world" and man's "wild longing for clarity" and order (*Myth* 28 and 21). Since death wipes everything out, what meaning can life possibly have? *Where* can values reside? It appears that, in the words of David Sprintzen:

> [W]e have been freed of *the illusion of hope* only to be plunged into a maelstrom in which *everything is permitted* and moral standards no longer have a leg to stand on. *Experiences are equivalent* so long as consciousness is present ... [Who] is to judge? (64 emphasis added)

Thus, there *can* be no moral basis on which to condemn someone who does decide to take his/her own life because he/she sees no point in living.

For Camus, acknowledging the absurdity of life is necessary for intellectual honesty, but merely *as a beginning*, not as an end in itself. The question, then, becomes: How can an absurd life nevertheless be *a meaningful life*? The obvious first step is to become *aware* of the absurd, to face the inevitability of death honestly. That is the theme of Camus' Cycle of the Absurd (*The Myth of Sisyphus*, *Caligula*, and *The Stranger*), which he termed works of negation. Put simply, while Jean-Paul Sartre's reaction to the experience of the absurd is nausea, Camus reacts with exhilaration

Camus, Mortality and Meaninglessness

Faith satisfies the human desire for life to have a transcendent meaning, but what of those for whom faith is no longer an option because they cannot believe in that wonderful place beyond the clouds which, in *Animal Farm* by George Orwell, Moses the Raven calls "Sugarcandy Mountain"? In a world without transcendent values, not only is suffering meaningless, but (more shockingly) so are pleasure, happiness, and apparently positive concepts such as love, justice and humanity. Once it is accepted that God is dead, and we are all mortal, then life is absurd.

At the age of seventeen, Albert Camus was diagnosed with tuberculosis, a disease for which there was, at that time, no cure. Camus had to face the real prospect that his life would be cut short at any moment. Catherine Brosman links Camus' diagnosis with his later development of the concept of the absurd, "To Camus, the absurd meant first of all the disparity between a young consciousness hungry for experience and crying out for meaning, and *a body condemned to illness, ultimately to death*" (22 emphasis added).

On an instinctive rather than on a conscious level, Meursault shares with Camus a heightened sense of his own mortality - the novel opens with the death of Meursault's mother. Unlike every other character in the novel, he appears, without ever having given it much thought, to assume: that the absurdity of life means that ethical conduct is an illusion; that since everything is permitted one choice is as good as another; and that human values are meaningless. Robert Zaretsky defines the reader's initial impression of the 'otherness' of Meursault thus:

> Meursault's life is not unique: many others have lived equally drab lives; many more have known far worse. What makes Meursault's life different is *his refusal or inability to hew it into meaningful narrative.* The traditional comforting formulas we impose on our life stories are absent here. Instead, life is one damn thing after another. There is no logic, no hierarchy of importance, no effort of synthesis. Like the clatter rising from the street below Meursault's terrace, *it signifies nothing.* (53 emphasis added)

Bespaloff expresses what it is that Meursault comes to understand, "Amid the indifference of a world devoid of God, nothing has any importance or value, *except* the pure act of living" (Brée ed. 95 emphasis added).

The novel ends without attempting to explore the questions which follow naturally: *How* should human beings respond to this reality? *How* should we live? *What* should we *do*? And most importantly of all to Camus: *How* should we relate to others? Camus, who was deeply concerned with ethical values and with establishing "a valid justification for life," would struggle with these questions for the rest of his life both as a political activist and as an artist (Rhein 33). His search for answers would lead to the personal and philosophical rift with existentialist Jean-Paul Sartre, and to the doomed struggle to find a viable moral and political position on the question of Algerian Independence. In Meursault's story, as in the other works of his Cycle of the Absurd, Camus aims to do no more than to establish a foundation upon which to examine questions which are still vitally important to every reader.

The Stranger by Albert Camus

The Stranger A Study Guide:

Learning aims:

Through studying this novel, you will:

1. experience one of the most original novels of the Twentieth Century and understand why it had such an impact upon its appearance;
2. explore the relationship between a novel and the author's philosophy.

Pre-reading:

This novel requires some pretty specialized vocabulary. Research the highlighted words. You will need a very good dictionary (or two!).

1. What is the normal meaning of **absurd**? What is the most absurd thing you have ever experienced? How is Camus' concept of the absurd different from the normal meaning of the word? (OK so the last question is difficult! Find a book on Camus and look on the Internet.)
2. What is the normal meaning of **existence**? What do you value (and not value) about your own existence? What beliefs about existence does the philosophy called **existentialism** hold? (OK another tough one, but I'm not expecting you to read a book on philosophy, just to get the basic idea.)
3. What is the difference between a person or an action that is **immoral** and one that is **amoral**? Give an example of each.
4. What is the normal meaning of **alienation**? Has there ever been a time when you have felt alienated from everyone (or nearly everyone) around you? Explain.

How to Use this Study Guide:

The questions are not designed to test you but to help you to locate and to understand information in the text. They do not normally have simple answers, nor is there always one answer. Consider a range of possibly interpretations - preferably by discussing the questions with others. Disagreement is encouraged!

Introduction:

We are now ready to look in detail at Camus' most detailed portrait of a man alienated from the values of the society in which he must live. Sprintzen describes the reader's first impressions of Meursault like this:

> Is not this Meursault a stranger to our normal feelings and expectations? We sense a distance. Not that he seeks to scandalize or offend. Far from it. He is rather quite unassuming, almost shy. He wants neither to offend nor to be hated. Expressing an air of naïveté, he often experiences an undercurrent of uneasiness as to what is expected of him. Occasionally he is moved to apologize without quite knowing

what he is guilty of. (23)

There is no satisfactory English rendering of the French title *L'Étranger*. The first English translation had the title *The Outsider*, but this was soon dropped in favor of the more literal *The Stranger*. However, as Akeroyd points out this lacks the force of the French that has more the sense of "The Foreigner" that much more accurately captures the protagonist's relationship to the French-Algerian society of which he is, perforce, a member, "He is a foreigner in a world which doesn't understand him and in which he frequently has experiences which make him feel a misfit" (30).

Meursault has responded to the sense that he lives in a universe that he cannot understand by adopting a philosophy of indifference; where they are in active (but self-destructive) revolt against an absurd life, Meursault is not. He senses the meaninglessness of life but does not live in the *consciousness* of that truth. Faced with an existence he does not understand, and surrounded by people who live their lives as though they *do* understand it, he simply does not think about it. Thus, Meursault lives a life reduced to experiencing existence as a succession of events from which he aims only to extract the maximum sensual gratification. Luppé explains:

> The central theme of the novel is the meaninglessness of Meursault's existence. His life has no purpose and no impulsion.; it proceeds blindly and automatically. It consists of movements, a sequence of half-thoughts and crude sensations ... Meursault is not an ordinary man, for he is without prejudices and without lies; *nor is he a rebel* for he has not discovered truly living values. He is the brute in man: the human creature stripped naked, in all his misery; Meursault is truth disclosed (43-4, 45 emphasis added)

Although he feels himself to be an alien in a society whose values, rituals and habits mean nothing to him, he is not in revolt against the absurd; he willing accepts powerlessness. He enjoys the physical pleasures of a young and presumably quite attractive *pied-noir*, and feels no resentment at having to spend nine hours a day working. That is to say, Meursault lives a natural life and appears fated to die a natural death. How this man comes to consciousness, how he comes to confront the absurd, is the central drama of the novel.

The Stranger by Albert Camus

PART ONE

Chapter 1

Meursault, the narrator and protagonist of the novel, is not Camus and neither is he Camus' spokesman. He narrates his story just before his execution for murder at a point where he understands its full significance, but his aim in the narrative is (with very few exceptions) to convey accurately his feelings at the time things happened.

Meursault is an office worker not a philosopher; as he later tells his lawyer, he has "pretty much lost the habit of analyzing [himself]" (65). As much as he would like others to believe that he is, Meursault is not "'the same as anyone'" (67). He regards emotions as meaningless abstractions – fictions invented by people to make themselves feel better by giving their lives the appearance of meaning. Thus, his inability to feel emotion is not a result of a psychological illness.

Deeply aware that he has a different world view from everyone else, Meursault spends most of his time trying to 'read' other people in order to know what is expected of him. However, he frequently misreads social situations causing him to feel embarrassed, inadequate and even guilty. He experiences life as a succession of unconnected sensual experiences, some pleasant and some unpleasant. As a result, he lives in the moment, almost completely unconcerned about either the past or the future.

1. Re-read paragraph one of the novel. It establishes Meursault as the narrator/protagonist. Comment on Meursault's reaction to the news of the death of his mother, and specifically on:
    a) his use of the informal, colloquial term "Maman" (very roughly 'mom' or 'mummy' rather than 'mother' which would be 'ma mère');
    b) the aspects of her death that *do* concern him;
    c) anything that you find lacking in his response;
    d) possible meanings (including those that the narrator may not intend) of his statement, "That doesn't mean anything" (3). To what exactly does "That" refer? (You should find three or four possible interpretations.);
    e) the writer's use of short sentences to reflect the narrator's state of mind.

2. Meursault concentrates throughout the chapter on practical details. These seem to interest him whereas social relationships appear to bore or even to antagonize him. Give examples of some of the practical details that capture his interest.

3. Meursault is often surprised or irritated by displays of emotion in others. Give examples. What do these have in common? How does this commonality explain his feelings? How does Meursault seek to block out emotion?

A Study Guide

4. Comment on the description of Pérez falling behind the coffin and finally fainting at the cemetery. Does Camus intend this to be comic? Does it have a symbolic interpretation?

5. In this chapter, Meursault repeatedly feels guilty or embarrassed. Give examples. What do these have in common? How does this commonality help the reader to understand his feelings?

6. Comment on the following dialogue between the nurse and Meursault, "She said, 'If you go slowly, you risk getting sunstroke. But if you go too fast, you work up a sweat and then catch a chill inside the church.' She was right. There was no way out" (17).This appears to be a comment on the heat of the day, but Meursault's conclusion suggests a more symbolic interpretation. Against what does Meursault feel there is "no way out"? (Note: He may or may not be conscious that his words carry this deeper meaning. What do you think?)

7. The chapter ends with Meursault listing a number of "images from that day that have stuck in my mind" (17-18). What do these have in common? What is the sole image that generates an *emotional* response in Meursault?

8. How do you react to Meursault's apparent lack of emotion about his mother's death? Is his seeming indifference a sign of honesty or lack of humanity or both?

Chapter 2

Meursault finds refuge from thought in practical details and logistics, which explains both why he is happy in his work and why he is such an efficient and productive employee. He feels most comfortable when he does not have to take decisions. Meursault's experience of being alive is limited to physical gratification and a daily routine of activities. He likes routine and hates having free-time.

In Marie, he appears to have found a companion who also lives exclusively for the gratification of her senses. They seem ideally suited because Meursault is no more capable of romantic love than he is capable of filial love. He is a stranger to the neighborhood in which he lives, observing but taking no part in the various social groups.

1. As the chapter opens, Meursault suddenly thinks that he understands why his boss was annoyed that he asked for two days off work. Comment on his use of the following expressions:
   a) "why my boss had seemed annoyed" (19);
   b) "naturally, my boss thought" (19);
   c) "that still doesn't keep me from understanding my boss's point of view" (19).

Find further examples in this chapter of Meursault apparently coming to an

The Stranger by Albert Camus

understanding of the feelings of other people.

2. Comment on the way in which Meursault describes his attraction for Marie, "I'd had a thing for her at the time" (19). How did he react to the end of their relationship?

3. What leads Meursault to comment of Marie, "she seemed very surprised" (Note that word "seemed" again!) and, "She gave a little start" (20)? Comment on Meursault's statement that his mother died, "'Yesterday'" (20). How does he respond when he notes Marie's reaction?

4. How does Meursault's description of his interactions with Marie on the beach and in the cinema indicate the importance he places on the physical aspects of existence?

5. Do you find Meursault's behavior on the day after his mother's funeral inappropriate? Why (or why not)?

6. What seems to you significant about the way in which Meursault describes the people whom he observes from his balcony? How is Meursault different from the "distinguished" man with his wife and children, the waiter doing his job, and the young soccer players (23)?

7. Comment on the sentence, "Then I thought maybe I ought to have some dinner" (24). What does it show about Meursault?

8. Based on your reading of this chapter, why do you think that Meursault does not like Sundays?

Chapter 3

Convinced that there are no transcendent values, Meursault lives in a valueless world. Faced with the cruel mathematics of human mortality, length of life is clearly of no importance: it doesn't matter when you die; it matters that you *will* die. Because of death, nothing in life can be of any lasting significance, and one choice is as good as another because there is no valid moral basis on which to evaluate them.

Strong-willed people live their lives in defiance of these two truths - or say rather, by ignoring them. Meursault, who lacks self-will, is vulnerable to such people because he is easily influenced. In terms of how he lives his life, this chapter probably shows the worst aspects of Meursault.

1. Meursault admits that he does not understand why his boss "seemed to be relieved" (25). What is it that he is failing to understand about his boss's reaction? What else about his boss does Meursault record without appearing to understand it? How does Meursault in a similar way fail to understand and respond appropriately to Céleste a little later in the chapter?

A Study Guide

2. Meursault reports that his boss said that the wet towel is "really a minor detail" (25). Why is it not minor to Meursault?

3. What does the incident in which Meursault and Emmanuel jump up on the truck tell us about Meursault? Look particularly at the language that is used to describe the incident.

4. Both Céleste and Raymond take a moral position on Salamano beating his dog. What is it? How does Meursault react?

5. Contrast the way in which "the neighborhood" regards Raymond with Meursault's attitude towards him. How do you explain the difference?

6. Why does Meursault agree to be Raymond's "pal"?

7. Raymond describes several acts of violence that he has committed. How does Camus bring home to the reader the seriousness of these through Raymond's own account? What is Meursault's reaction to hearing about them?

8. Why does Meursault agree to assist in Raymond's scheme to get revenge on his mistress? Comment on the use of adjectives in the following description, "he took out a sheet of paper, a *yellow* envelope, a *small red* pen box, and a *square* bottle with *purple* ink in it" (32 emphasis added).

9. At the end of the chapter, Meursault thinks, "[Raymond said] that it was one of those things that was bound to happen sooner or later. I thought so too" (33). What similarities, and what differences, do you find between the views of life and death held by Meursault and by Raymond?

Chapter 4

Meursault's relationship with Marie appears to combine the maximum of sensual gratification with the minimum of emotional commitment which makes him happy and leads Meursault to feel that he is living in harmony with the physical world. However, although he is currently unaware of it, Marie's love for Meursault threatens to change completely the nature of their relationship. Similarly, becoming a "pal" to Raymond Sintès carries obligations the nature of which Meursault entirely fails to understand. Thus, Meursault's relationships with Marie and Sintès threaten to destroy the independence from society which is the basis of his life as a stranger.

Salamano's relationship with his dog is a habit (a routine) which makes it easier for the old man to avoid thinking about the reality of death.

1. What expression does Meursault use twice to describe his attraction to Marie? What does it tell you about him?

2. "A minute later she asked me if I loved her. I told her it didn't mean anything

The Stranger by Albert Camus

but that I didn't think so" (35). Is Meursault's reaction to Marie's question honest or insensitive? Perhaps you feel it is both?

3. Contrast the reactions of Meursault and Marie to the incident involving Raymond, the woman, and the policeman. How is Meursault's reaction to the beaten woman similar to his reaction to Marie's question?

4. Comment on the unconscious irony of Meursault's conclusion, "I found him very friendly with me and I thought it was a nice moment" (38).

5. When Meursault hears Mr. Salamano crying, he comments, "For some reason I thought of Maman" (39). Explain what it is that he is failing to understand.

6. What is significant about Meursault's eating and sleeping in this chapter?

Chapter 5

Meursault is losing the autonomy and isolation which his life had before the death of his mother: his involvement with Sintès drags him into a family feud which has racial overtones; his boss's offer of a promotion threatens to disrupt Meursault's easy-going, physical Algerian life-style; and Marie's proposal that they get married threatens to take away his independence.

The robot-woman and Salamano each epitomize unsatisfactory and inauthentic responses to the absurdity of human mortality. Salamano exerts upon Meursault the pressures of social expectations to which he is expected to conform.

1. Why do you think that Meursault has no desire to live in Paris? What does the boss find unsatisfactory about Meursault's reaction to his offer? (Comment on Meursault's expression, "He looked upset" [41].)

2. "Then she pointed out that marriage was a serious thing. I said, 'No'" (42). Explain why Marie and Meursault have such a different view of marriage. Why does Marie decide that she wants to marry Meursault despite this difference of opinion?

3. What is significant about Meursault's reaction to the "strange little woman" at Céleste's (43)? [Note that this character will reappear later to watch Meursault's trial and appear to judge him.]

4. Comment on the following aspects of Meursault's dialogue with Salamano:
   a) the way in which Salamano tries to impose some meaning on Meursault's life and actions;
   b) the theme of the inevitability of decay and death;
   c) Meursault's reaction on learning that some people had been critical of his decision to put his mother in a home.

A Study Guide

5. Without his narrator being aware of it, Camus has set up a conflict that will have a catastrophic impact on Meursault's life. Trace the way in which this has been developed in the novel.

Chapter 6

Understanding this chapter is central to understanding the novel as a whole, and a satisfactory reading must explain the significance of the sun in a consistent way. Meursault alternates between feeling that the sun is an antagonist and feeling that it is a benevolent force. Both perceptions are fundamental errors. Meursault feels happy when he is free to enjoy the sensual pleasures of the day, but unhappy when placed under pressure by other characters to conform to their expectations, thus he projects his feelings onto his environment – specifically he anthropomorphizes the sun. This is a fundamental mistake.

Meursault comes to understand that man is entirely free to choose his actions. Given man's mortality, he realizes that one choice is the same as another. He goes back to the spring to find a refuge from the "strains" of both the social and the physical worlds. He perceives the sun as an antagonist because he unconsciously sees it as an embodiment of the pressures which are making his life intolerable (his obligations to Raymond and to Marie). Having escaped the pressures of society, he encounters on the beach the most fundamental of these pressures in his growing awareness of his own mortality in contrast to the immortality of the physical world.

Meursault shoots the Arab as an act of defiance, of self-destructive revolt. The shooting is Meursault's conscious rejection of happiness; it is a form of suicide and as such it is an evasion of the absurd.

1. Comment on the simile "the day, already bright with sun, hit me like a slap in the face" (47). How does it foreshadow the dramatic events that will happen at the beach?

2. In what ways is Meursault's comment on Raymond's white hairy arms, "I found it a little repulsive" typical of him (47-8)? (Compare it with his complaint about towels in the washroom at work and contrast it with his failure to make any judgment about Raymond's immorality.)

3. How does Camus make the encounter with the Arabs by the tobacconist's shop ominous?

4. How does Meursault's description of his first visit to the beach and of swimming with Marie emphasize the way in which he enjoys the natural environment?

5. How does Meursault's description of the natural environment (particularly the sun and the sand) differ when he gives an account of walking on the beach after

The Stranger by Albert Camus

lunch? (Show how Camus' use of language becomes more ornate, featuring such rhetorical devices as personification and metaphor, and contrasting strongly with the spare, simple descriptions that Meursault usually offers.)

6. What is typical about Meursault's role in the first violent encounter with the two Arabs and his reaction to the women when the men have returned to the house?

7. Meursault makes a number of judgments in this chapter. Comment on the validity of the following:
    a) "It was then that I realized that you could either shoot or not shoot" (56);
    b) "But the heat was so intense that it was just as bad standing still ... To stay or go, it amounted to the same thing ... I turned back toward the beach" (57);
    c) "As far as I was concerned, the whole thing was over, and I'd gone there without even thinking about it" (58).

8. Why does Meursault go to the beach the third time?

9. Why does Meursault fire the first shot at the Arab?

10. Why does he then fire four times into the man's inert body?

11. Is his reaction to what he has done typical or untypical of him?

A Study Guide

PART TWO

> The meaning of the book lies precisely in the parallelism of the two parts. Conclusion: society needs people who weep at their mother's funeral; or else one is never condemned for the crime one thinks. Moreover, I see ten other possible conclusions. (*Notebooks 1942-1951*, March 1942, 19)

Chapter 1

In a number of ways, Part Two is a very different kind of novel from Part One. Despite the detailed depiction of ordinary life in Part One, it becomes clear immediately that in Part Two Camus is not writing a realistic novel of Colonial Algeria. One aspect of this is that the focus of the investigation quickly shifts away from the murder of the Arab to Meursault's reaction to the death of his mother. He will be tried for the way he lived his life in Part One.

Meursault is also a rather different character being much more assertive and unapologetic about the way he lives his life than at any point in Part One. Camus manipulates the reader to see Meursault as the victim of an arbitrary and invalid process, and to do this the Arab has to disappear. In two interviews, the values and beliefs of humanism and Catholicism are subjected to Meursault's criticism and found to be wanting.

Meursault is forced by the questions of both his defense counsel and the magistrate to reflect upon the way in which he has led his life.

1. Give examples of the way in which Meursault focuses on the practical details of his life in prison rather than on its emotional elements. How does this tendency lead him to make a number of responses that are inappropriate to his situation?

2. How does Meursault answer the charge that he "had 'shown insensitivity' the day of Maman's funeral" (64)?

3. Meursault frequently claims that he is "like everyone else ... the same as anyone" (66, 67). How do the people to whom he is saying this react? How do you react? Is he right?

4. What reasons does Meursault give for failing to respond to being questioned about the pause between the first and second shots that he fired at the Arab?

5. On being asked by the magistrate if he is sorry for murdering the Arab man, Meursault replies "that more than sorry I felt kind of annoyed. I got the impression he didn't understand" (70). Explain what Meursault means.

6. Explain how Meursault's atheism and his indifference to his mother's death challenge the magistrate's belief in a rational world controlled by God - a belief

that gives his life meaning. In what way does the magistrate adapt to this perceived challenge so that he is soon able to treat Meursault in a cordial way.

Chapter 2

This chapter is written from the perspective of Meursault at the end of the chapter not that of the Meursault at the end of the novel. As a character, Meursault appears more sympathetic because of his child-like inability to understand the situation he is in.

The interview with Marie is a failure ironically in a room full of people who are communicating successfully.

One important effect of prison is to wean Meursault off his addiction to sensual gratification, but becoming reconciled to the reality of prison is not the positive development which Meursault as narrator presents it as being. Meursault is, almost despite himself, becoming more self-aware, but until he faces the reality of his imminent death he is still evading the human situation.

1. What is the difference between Meursault's experience of prison before and after his one visit from Marie?

2. What are the physical aspects of confinement that weigh most heavily on Meursault's mind? Explain his comment, "I shouldn't exaggerate ... it was easier for me than for others" (76).

3. What humor does Camus get out of Meursault's delayed understanding of why he is in prison? (See 78)

4. Meursault comments that the story of the Czech murdered by his own mother and sister was "perfectly natural" (80). What does he mean by this?

5. Where has he used this word before in the novel?

6. What was it that the Nurse said at Maman's funeral? Why does Meursault see this statement as relevant to his prison experience? What is he beginning to realize about the events that led up to the murder and the murder itself?

Chapter 3

Although the procedures of the trial are realistically presented (Camus spent some years as a court reporter), the way in which the focus is shifted to an examination of the way Meursault has lived his life in Part One is allegory not realism.

Camus' essential criticism of the trial is that the plausible interpretations which are imposed onto Meursault's conduct in Part One are palpably false.

By the end of this chapter, Meursault has understood that love, happiness and contentment can give life value; he has still not yet understood that man's freedom to choose how to live his life can actually be meaningful even if

A Study Guide

existence lacks transcendent values (e.g. God).

1. Before the trial starts, what evidence is there that Meursault totally underestimates the seriousness of his situation? Meursault's comments indicate that he feels himself to be a detached observer rather than a person on trial for his life. Which of his comments give you this impression?

2. Comment on the unconscious irony of Meursault's reaction to being asked his name, age, date of birth, etc., "I realized it was only natural, because it would be a very serious thing to try the wrong man" (87).

3. What rational explanation of Meursault's crime is offered by the prosecution and how does the testimony of the witnesses add support to it?

4. How does Meursault's perception of himself in relation to the trial change as the case proceeds, and it becomes increasingly clear that he will be found guilty? Comment particularly on his statements:
   a) "I had this stupid urge to cry because I could feel how much all these people hated me" (90);
   b) "I felt a stirring go through the room and for the first time I realized that I was guilty" (90);
   c) "it was the first time in my life I ever wanted to kiss a man" (93).

[The following comment from Spark Notes is *very* helpful: "Meursault comes to understand that his failure to interpret or find meaning in his own life has left him vulnerable to others, who will impose such meaning for him. Until this point, Meursault has unthinkingly drifted from moment to moment, lacking the motivation or ability to examine his life as a narrative with a past, present, and future. Even during the early part of the trial he watches as if everything were happening to someone else. Only well into the trial does Meursault suddenly realize that the prosecutor has successfully manufactured an interpretation of Meursault's life, and that, in the jury's eyes, he likely appears guilty."]

5. What does Meursault's lawyer mean when he says of the trial, "'everything is true and nothing is true!'" (91).

6. Comment on Meursault's closing statement, "No, there was no way out, and no one can imagine what nights in prison are like" (81).

Chapter 4

The legal system finds Meursault to be a "monster" (102), but this chapter subjects that system to withering satire. In their summations the prosecutor and the defender each construct a false identity for Meursault: he finds the prosecutor's argument "plausible" (99) and "right" (100), but the reader knows it to be untrue. Meursault himself feels entirely excluded from the trial, but given

The Stranger by Albert Camus

an opportunity to speak he can offer no explanation for the way he has lived his life. Meursault still does not grasp the real consequences of a guilty verdict.

Meursault develops a conscious and intense appreciation for the "lasting joys" of a life which he formerly took for granted and which he has now lost forever (104).

1. What does Meursault find interesting about hearing people talk about himself? Why does hearing them soon lead to a return of his feeling of disengagement from the court proceedings ("they seemed to be arguing the case as if it had nothing to do with me" [98])?

2. What does he find "plausible" and consistent in the prosecution's account of his actions?

3. How does the prosecution succeed in linking Meursault's case to the trial of a man for parricide (the killing of a father) that will follow it?

4. How does Meursault respond to his lawyer's use of first person narrative to present Meursault's motives to the jury?

5. At the start of the chapter, Meursault asks, "were the two speeches [those of the prosecution and the defense] so different after all?" (98). What do they have in common in relation to Meursault?

6. What is unusual, as compared with most defendants, about Meursault's reaction to his lawyer's explanation that there is very little chance of "overturning the verdict" (106)?

7. Show how, near the end of both Chapters 3 and 4, Meursault becomes aware of the life-experiences that he has lost as a result of his actions. Comment on the irony of this realization.

Chapter 5

Although they do not admit it, most people find the idea of a death in which "nothing remains" to be a "terrifying ordeal" causing "extreme despair ... more than a man can bear" (117). At the start of this chapter, Meursault also feels this terror of death - now that he has been sentenced to execution, he has no alternative but to face the ultimate reality. Meursault eventually sees that extending one's life-span does not change the fact of mortality since all men have "only a little time left" even if they are going to live for another twenty years, and we should not waste it on things which do not interest us (120).

Meursault realizes that he was right to believe that we are all free to live the life we choose, but that he has mistaken the nature of man's relationship with the world, and now feels that the pursuit of individual happiness gives life value. The world is not against us; it is indifferent. We are entirely free: we have the

A Study Guide

privilege of life. Understanding what he now understands, Meursault would not have shot the Arab.

1. At the start of this chapter, Meursault says, "All I care about right now is escaping the machinery of justice, seeing if there's any way out of the inevitable" (108). How has his attitude regressed since the end of the trial?

2. What does Meursault mean when he says that "there really was something ridiculously out of proportion between the verdict such certainty was based on and the imperturbable march of events from the moment the verdict was announced" (109)? (Note how differently Meursault speaks here as compared with his narrative style in Part One. He is here reflecting on causality.)

3. In what ways is hope a barrier that Meursault must overcome before he can come to terms with the reality of his own death?

4. By what difficult (but accurate) reasoning does Meursault persuade himself finally "to accept [the idea] of the rejection of my appeal" (114)?

5. How does the chaplain give meaning to his own life? How does Meursault react to the philosophy (or theology) that the chaplain urges him to accept?

6. Following his confrontation with the chaplain, Meursault experiences an epiphany, "I was sure about me, about everything ... sure of my life and sure of the death I had waiting me ... I had been right, I was still right, I was always right" (120-1). He gets it! Understanding this epiphany is the key to understanding Camus' message, his purpose in writing the book, and his absurdist philosophy. (Camus always rejected the label 'existentialist,' but critics have continued to apply it to his thinking.)
    a) Meursault goes on to ask repeatedly the rhetorical question, "What did it matter ...?" (121) Explain why none of the things that he considers matters.
    b) What does Meursault mean when he says, "Everyone was privileged. There were only privileged people" (121)? (*Note:* We are *not* just privileged because we have been born and so given a life. There is more to it than that.)
    c) What does he mean when he refers to the chaplain as "this condemned man" (122)? Why is his use of this word ironic?

7. Look carefully at the final paragraph of the novel:
    a) Now that Meursault has accepted that, "Nothing, nothing mattered" (121), how does he react to the physical beauties of the world he is about to leave?
    b) How does he explain his mother's taking a "fiancé" at the end of her life?
    c) What does he mean when he says of his mother, "Nobody, nobody had

      the right to cry over her" (122)?
- d) What does he mean by the oxymoron "the *gentle indifference* of the world ... so like a brother, really" (122-3 emphasis added)?
- e) Why does he want to die with "a large crowd of spectators ... [who will] greet me with cries of hate" (123)?

8. Spark Notes makes the comment that at the end of the novel Meursault comes to understand "the redemptive value of abandoning hope." Comment on the meaning of this paradox.

After Word

Camus himself came to feel that *The Stranger* placed too much emphasis on the individual and that a "different order of understanding and ethics was necessary, one that encompassed others rather than isolating the individual subject. Society, not the individual, was now the measure of meaning" (Zaretsky 58). Writing in 1955 to the critic Roland Barthes, Camus made a distinction between *The Stranger*, which he said represented "*révolte solitaire*," and *The Plague* which he saw as a transition to the recognition of community (Lottman 543). Indeed, he would eventually write in his *cahiers*, "I see clearly that absurd thought ... ends in an impasse, and the problem is, Can one live in an impasse?" (quoted in Todd 167). This explains Camus' own involvement as an engaged artist in the political and social questions of his day.

The final words belong to Albert Camus:

> If we assume that nothing has any meaning, then we must conclude that the world is absurd. But does nothing have a meaning? I have never believed that we can remain at this point. Even as I was writing *The Myth of Sisyphus* I was thinking about the essay on revolt that I would write later on, in which I would attempt, after having described the different aspects of the feeling of the Absurd, to describe the different attitudes of man in revolt. ("Encounter with Albert Camus" *Essays.* 356)

A Study Guide

Post-Reading

I highly recommend watching the movie *The Stranger* (1967) directed by Luchino Visconti which is available on the Internet. The following thoughts may prove useful.

In 1967, seven years after Camus' death, Italian film director Luchino Visconti released *The Stranger* starring Marcello Mastroianni as Arthur Meursault and Anna Karina as Marie Cardona. The film was nominated for The Golden Lion, the highest prize given at the Venice Film Festival, but it was neither a critical nor a financial success on its release and has become one of the director's forgotten films whilst maintaining a cult following. Perhaps this failure is because this film is so different from Visconti's normal style, but I suspect that it has more to do with the essentially undramatic nature of Camus' novel. Visconti himself pointed to conflict between his own vision for the film which would have been based on selected scenes from the novel and that of Camus' widow, Francine, who rejected the first screenplay because it was not entirely faithful to the text. Visconti told *Le Monde*, "*The Stranger* became a fiasco because Albert Camus' widow demanded objective, absurd fidelity. In order to honor our contract I was forced to renounce the film I had always wanted to do and to confine myself strictly to the text" (quoted in Gay-Crosier 168).

The film begins after Meursault's arrest as he is being taken in handcuffs to his initial interrogation. The magistrate asks him if he has a lawyer, and Meursault replies that he does not think it is necessary because "I think my defense is quite simple." This is immediately followed by a flashback to Meursault running to catch the bus to Marengo. In this way, the film establishes Meursault as a commentator on the action of Part One of the novel with the expectation that his commentary will present Meursault's "simple" defense. The commentary is delivered in a series of voiceovers which stick pretty closely to the text of the novel. Thus the film's narrative perspective is very different from that of the novel in which Meursault narrates from the beginning from the perspective of a condemned man following his final epiphany.

The film immediately establishes the heat and the oppressively bright light of the Algerian summer. Exterior shots are suffused with a bleaching white light, and sweat-marks are evident on clothing. An exception is the scene at the pool when Meursault meets Marie. Meursault comments that the day is "mild" and that "the sky filled my head with blue and gold." The scenes follow Part One of the novel quite faithfully, the most significant addition being a strain of eerie music which plays whenever Meursault feels under particular stress or when he feels uncomfortably dissociated from his surroundings. A sustained example is when Meursault and Marie are lying on the sand the Sunday they spend at Masson's house. Marie is commenting on the Boss's offer of a move to Paris

The Stranger by Albert Camus

which Meursault has already rejected. Marie says, "I was thinking. Why not tell your boss that you have just reconsidered everything he said and accept that job in Paris next year. I'd come with you naturally. I'm dying to see Paris." The music shows that Meursault is sensing the pressure which their relationship is exerting to limit his freedom.

In depicting the three confrontations on the beach, the ominous music builds to a climax, and the bleaching white of the sun robs the scene of most of its color. As he returns to the beach alone, Meursault is shown to be suffering from the extreme heat; his shirt, saturated with sweat, clings to his back. The firing of the first shot is presented as an instinctive reaction to the reflection of the sun off of the Arab's knife; Meursault immediately looks shocked and disbelieving at what he has done. The remaining four shots are, however, clearly a separate and deliberate act. Meursault's commentary establishes that they are not the result of dissociation or confusion, "I shook off the veil of sweat and light that had blinded me." Rather, they are presented as deliberate acts designed to punish himself, "I realized that I had shattered the impassive stillness of the afternoon and the shimmering silence of the beach. And so I fired again." The paradoxical nature of the shots is that by an act of deliberate choice, Meursault places himself in a position where he will no longer have choice, "Four shots like four fateful raps on the door to my destiny."

As the action reaches the point at which the film began, no further rationale is given to explain Meursault as narrator; he simply continues to fulfill that role, though from what perspective it is not clear. The interrogation scenes establish the court officials as unsympathetic, even grotesque, characters who find Meursault both inexplicable and offensive. The magistrate appears almost demented when brandishing the crucifix in Meursault's face and demanding that he accept Christ's sacrifice.

The dialogue of the trial sticks very closely to the novel, but in presenting the trial in visual terms the emphasis on Meursault being tried for the way he lived his life (his failure to love his mother and to respond appropriately to her death, and his associating with the criminal Sintès) to the virtual exclusion of the actual shooting of the Arab becomes very clear. Not a single Arab is shown in the courtroom. The court officials are presented as grotesque and the court proceedings as anachronistic. The helpless frustration of Meursault as he hears himself discussed is clear, as is his inability to explain his action in firing the shots when he is given the opportunity to do so. The scene where the guilty verdict is given is particularly telling: the judges are wearing symbolic black and red robes which seem to be from a previous century, and the chief judge wears comic-looking *pince nez* to read the verdict in language which is ridiculously formal and official.

The director's problem with the concluding scenes in the jail is a more extreme version of the problems posed by filming the entire novel: *The Stranger* is the story of Meursault's intellectual growth. The drama is psychological, and as such it is virtually impossible to present Camus' meaning in terms of action. Visconti addresses this challenge in two ways. Firstly, Meursault's thoughts are presented in extended voiceovers, and secondly the important series of temptations through which Meursault passes are compressed in a short sequence of two minutes during which Meursault passes from being terrified that the guards will come for him to understanding that "it makes very little difference whether one dies at the age of thirty or at the age of seventy for once you're dead it doesn't matter how or when you died."

The climactic scene with the chaplain is, of course, more dramatic though their conflict is one of philosophy so their dialogue tends to be rather wordy. The chaplain comes across as a sympathetic character, but also a weak one: it is clear that, when he speaks of every person having doubts about their certainties, he is unconsciously speaking of his own fragile faith. Meursault's final epiphany is presented very powerfully in voiceover. He has no sooner understood that happiness is possible in life than the guards enter the cell, bind his hands behind his back, and take Meursault to execution.

The Stranger by Albert Camus

Glossary
(of words you will find useful in discussing this novel)

first-person narrator/narrative - The narrative in a prose work may either be third or first person. Third person narrative is told by an unidentified voice which belongs to someone not directly involved in the events narrated. First person narrative means that story is told from the necessarily limited viewpoint of one of the characters writing or speaking directly about themselves and their experience.

image - Imagery is a blanket term that describes the use of figurative language to represent objects, actions and ideas in such a way that it appeals to our five physical senses. Thus, amongst others, similes, metaphors and symbolism are examples of images.

> ***metaphor*** - A metaphor is a implied comparison in which whatever is being described is referred to as though it were another thing (e.g., "To be, or not to be: that is the question: / Whether 'tis nobler in the mind to suffer / The *slings and arrows* of outrageous *fortune*, / Or to take arms against *a sea of troubles*, / And by opposing end them?" Shakespeare *Hamlet*)
>
> ***simile*** - A simile is a descriptive comparison which uses the words "like" or "as" to make the intended comparison clear (e.g., "O my Luve's like a red, red rose / That's newly sprung in June; / O my Luve's like the melodie / That's sweetly play'd in tune." Robert Burns).
>
> ***symbol*** - A description in which one thing stand for or represents or suggests something bigger and more significant than itself. Normally a material object is used to represent an idea, belief, action, theme, person, etc. (e.g., in the Burns poem above, he uses the rose because it is a traditional symbol for love, passion, emotion and romance just as the sun became a natural and almost universal symbol of kingship).

irony / ironic - The essential feature of irony is the presence of a contradiction between an action or expression and the meaning it has in the context in which it occurs. Writers are always conscious of using irony, but their characters may either be aware or unaware that something that they say or do is ironic.

A Study Guide

Appendix 1: A Structure for Understanding The Stranger Part 2, Chapter 5.

In this chapter, Meursault suffers a series of temptations. (Camus obviously has in mind the temptations of Christ.) In Meursault's case, he is tempted to hope: the hope of extending his life works against his confrontation with the reality of his mortality. Only once Meursault has accepted that the reality of death is not affected by the length of a man's life can he become understand the privilege that is life. The graphic below identifies the stages of Meursault's developing understanding.

Page 108-109

The machinery of society   v   The hope of the imagination

Page 109-110

The way the verdict was reached   v   The very serious consequences
(random, trivial, absurd)

Page 110

Imagining he is watching   v   Actually being the person
an execution   executed

The Stranger by Albert Camus

Page 111-112

The romantic notion of execution   v The simple efficiency of execution

Page 112-113

Imagination of the coming of dawn   v

Page 113-114

The hope of 20 more years of life   v

Page 114-115

The hope of a pardon   v

Page 115-120

v

Appendix 2: The Trial of Meursault

The following class/group activity will be useful to teachers. I have the class prepare and present the trial before we begin reading Part Two. As far as possible, arrange students in groups of three: one to play the witness, one the prosecutor, and one the defense. Suggest that, since there is no doubt that Meursault shot the Arab, the trial will be more about his character. Have groups work to develop the best questions and answers for each side, and practice their scene. When the groups have finished preparing (perhaps one hour), the trial can take place. I usually act as judge just to keep things moving along. The trial normally takes an hour.

The charge: The accused, Meursault, is charged with the premeditated murder of an Arab citizen of Algeria for which the punishment is execution by guillotine.

Witnesses for the prosecution: The Director, The Caretaker, Thomas Pérez, Marie Cardona, The Chaplain.

Witnesses for the defense: Céleste, Salamano, Raymond Sintès, Meursault.

The function of the lawyers for the prosecution:

The prosecution will aim to show that the murder of the Arab is only the last of a series of actions which show the indifference of the accused to the moral values of society. The prosecution will aim to show Meursault as a man lacking normal human emotions and generally accepted moral values: they will seek to convict him for the way in which he led his life before the shooting as much as for the shooting itself.

The function of the lawyers for the defense:

Since there is no doubt that Meursault fired the fatal shots, the defense can only hope to provide mitigating circumstances in the hope of avoiding the death penalty. The defense will aim to show Meursault as a loving son, a popular and efficient worker, and a good neighbor. They will try to separate the shooting from what went before it and explain the shooting as the result of provocation and extreme mental agitation brought on by the situation.

The Stranger by Albert Camus

Order of proceedings:

1. The judge will read the charge and ask the accused to record a plea.
2. The prosecution will make an opening statement.
3. The defense will make an opening statement.
4. Witnesses for the prosecution will be called.
5. Witnesses for the defense will be called.
6. The prosecution will make a concluding statement.
7. The defense will make a concluding statement.
8. The judge will direct the jury.
9. The jury will deliver a verdict.

A Study Guide

Witnesses for the prosecution:	*Witnesses for the defense:*
The Director	Céleste
The Caretaker	Salamano
Thomas Pérez	Raymond Sintès
Marie Cardona	Meursault's boss
The Chaplain	Meursault

The Stranger by Albert Camus

Appendix 3: Graphic organizers
#1: Plot

Plot graph for *The Stranger*

- EXPOSITION
- RISING ACTION / CONFLICT
- CLIMAX
- FALLING ACTION / DENOUEMENT
- RESOLUTION

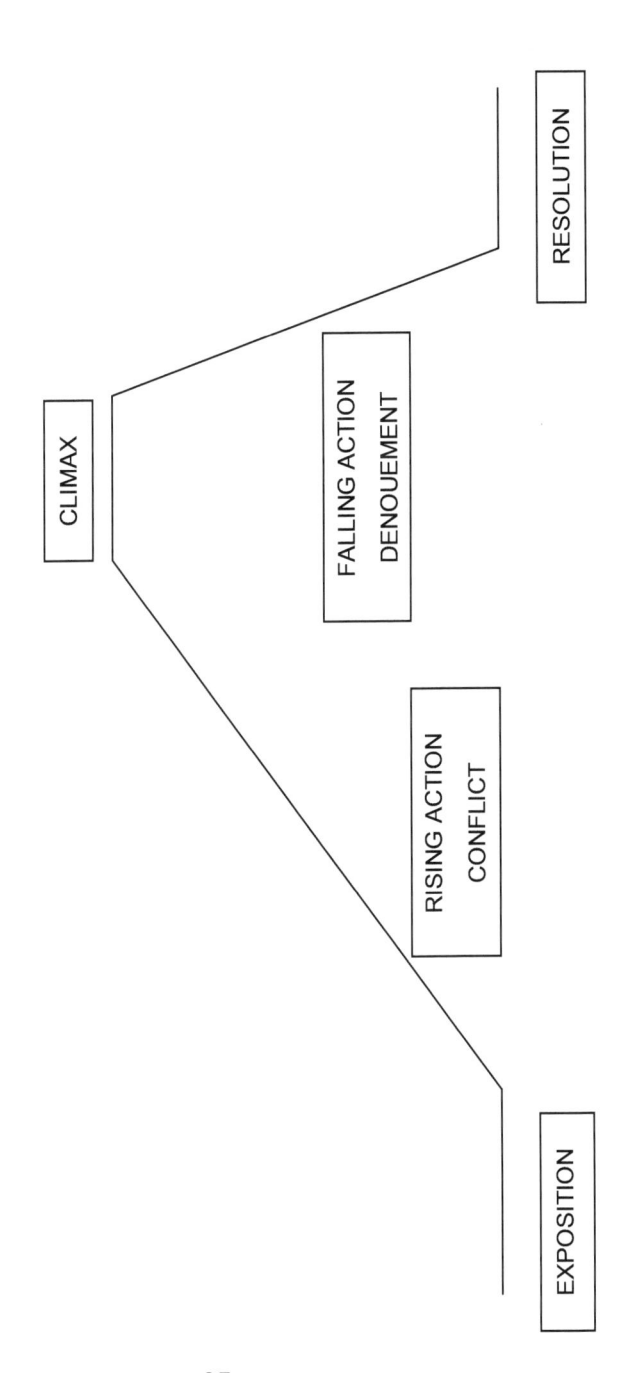

A Study Guide

#2: Different perspectives on the situation which initiates the action in the novel

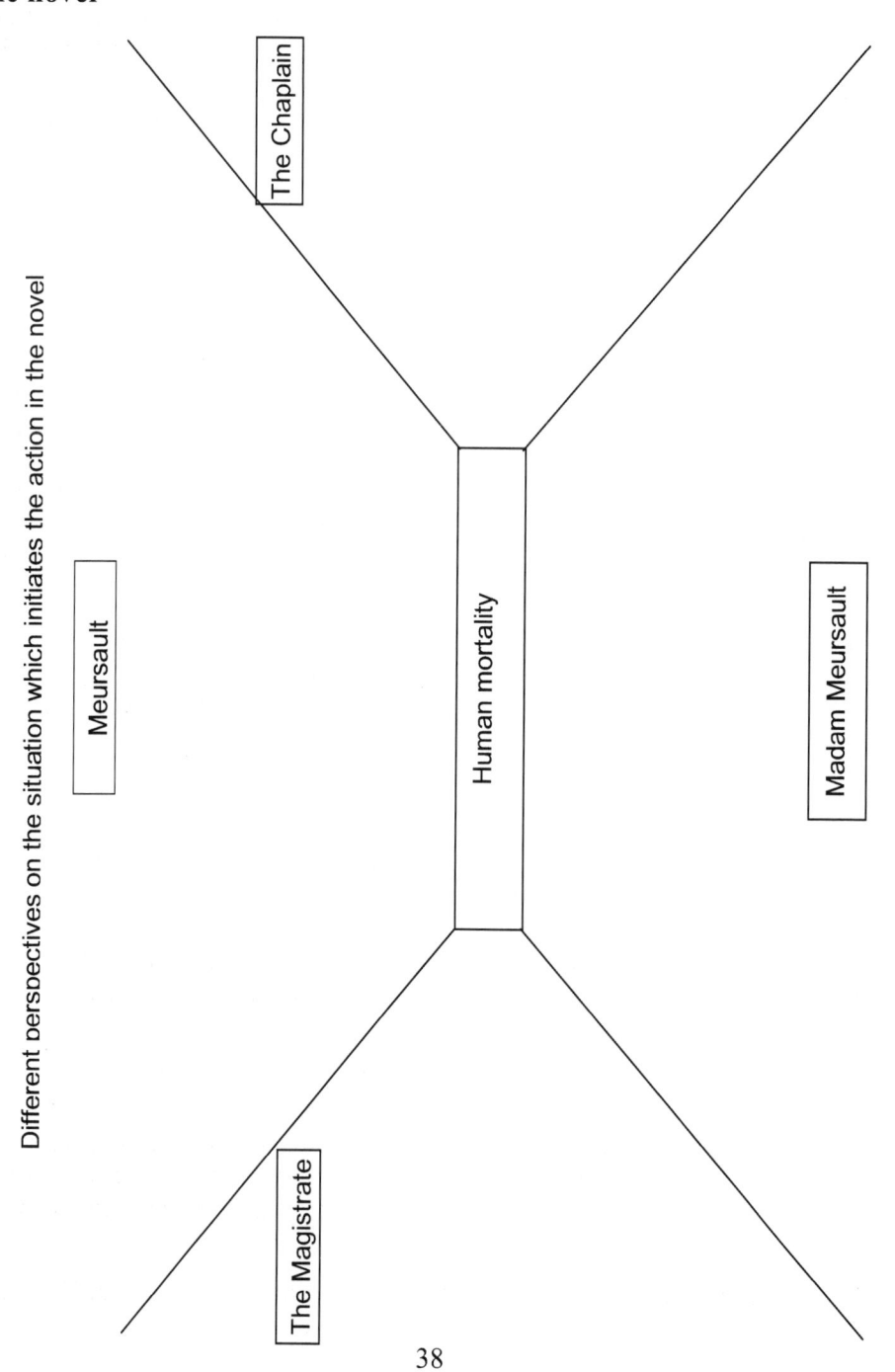

Different perspectives on the situation which initiates the action in the novel

- The Chaplain
- Meursault
- Human mortality
- Madam Meursault
- The Magistrate

The Stranger by Albert Camus

Appendix 4: Classroom Use of the Study Guide Questions

Although there are both closed and open questions in the Study Guide, very few of them have simple, right or wrong answers. They are designed to encourage in-depth discussion, disagreement, and (eventually) consensus. Above all, they aim to encourage students to go to the text to support their conclusions and interpretations.

I am not so arrogant as to presume to tell teachers how they should use this resource. I used it in the following ways, each of which ensured that students were well prepared for class discussion and presentations.

1. Set a reading assignment for the class and tell everyone to be aware that the questions will be the focus of whole class discussion the next class.

2. Set a reading assignment for the class and allocate particular questions to sections of the class (e.g. if there are four questions, divide the class into four sections, etc.).
In class, form discussion groups containing one person who has prepared each question and allow time for feedback within the groups.
Have feedback to the whole class on each question by picking a group at random to present their answers and to follow up with class discussion.

3. Set a reading assignment for the class, but do not allocate questions.
In class, divide students into groups and allocate to each group one of the questions related to the reading assignment the answer to which they will have to present formally to the class.
Allow time for discussion and preparation.

4. Set a reading assignment for the class, but do not allocate questions.
In class, divide students into groups and allocate to each group one of the questions related to the reading assignment.
Allow time for discussion and preparation.
Now reconfigure the groups so that each group contains at least one person who has prepared each question and allow time for feedback within the groups.

5. Before starting to read the text, allocate specific questions to individuals or pairs. (It is best not to allocate all questions to allow for other approaches and variety. One in three questions or one in four seems about right.) Tell students that they will be leading the class discussion on their question. They will need to start with a brief presentation of the issues and then conduct a question and answer session. After this, they will be expected to present a brief review of the discussion.

6. Having finished the text, arrange the class into groups of 3, 4 or 5. Tell each

A Study Guide

group to select as many questions from the Study Guide as there are members of the group.

Each individual is responsible for drafting out a written answer to one question, and each answer should be a substantial paragraph.

Each group as a whole is then responsible for discussing, editing and suggesting improvements to each answer, which is revised by the original writer and brought back to the group for a final proof reading followed by revision.

This seems to work best when the group knows that at least some of the points for the activity will be based on the quality of all of the answers.

Appendix 5: Guide to Further Reading

Todd, Olivier. *Albert Camus: A Life.*

A detailed and clear biography. The emphasis throughout is on Camus the man and the writer, largely leaving the reader to make connections between biography and the interpretation of individual works.

Showalter Jr., English. *"The Stranger" Humanity and the Absurd.*

Equally satisfies the needs of the general reader and of the advanced student. It provides a clear reading of the novel taking a thematic (rather than chapter-by-chapter) approach.

Gay-Crosier, Raymond. *Literary Masterpieces Volume 8: "The Stranger".*

Beautifully produced. Comprehensively places the novel in its biographical, historical and cultural context. The chapter analyzing the novel stresses the "inescapable ambiguity" of the text rather than offering one reading (95). The review of the critical responses to the novel since its publication will interest the advanced student.

Brosman, Catherine. *Literary Masters Volume 8: Albert Camus.*

Beautifully produced. Also comprehensively places Camus' works in their biographical, historical and cultural context. The more general scope of the book allows relatively little space for analysis of *The Stranger* itself.

McCarthy, Patrick. *Camus "The Stranger": A Student Guide.*

Uses the original French text with McCarthy's translation. The book places the novel in the context of Camus' life and of his cultural, political, and philosophical background and evaluates it using a range of critical approaches appropriate to the advanced student. McCarthy's central thesis is that, because of the incongruity between Part One and Part Two, the novel "resists interpretation" (79).

Bloom, Harold, ed. *Albert Camus's "The Stranger".*

Contains a 'Summary and Analysis' section which is rather more summary than analysis. The book also gives ten selected critical readings which are much more useful though rather short.

SparkNotes on *The Myth of Sisyphus* **and** *The Stranger.*

Teachers are often reluctant to bring these (and other similar notes) to the attention of their students fearing, with some justification, that the students will read the notes rather than the texts themselves. Like all secondary sources, they should be used critically as an aid to forming your own conclusions.

Kamel Daoud *The Meursault Investigation* (2015)

This novel gives the Arab version of the murder committed by French-Algerian Meursault in Albert Camus' *The Stranger* (1942). In a bar in Oran, Algeria, Harun, an old Arab man, tells an unnamed French listener about the crucial point in his own life and in the life of his mother. In 1942, when he was seven, his older brother, Musa, was shot on an Algiers beach in the glaring midday sun by a French-Algerian called Meursault. Meursault was quickly arrested and subsequently tried and sentenced to be executed. Before his death, however, Meursault wrote a first-person account of the weeks leading up to the murder, the actual shooting and the judicial process which led to his conviction and sentencing. This account was subsequently published, and the writing was so brilliant that everyone focused on Meursault and forgot that the real victim in the case was the unnamed Arab whom he killed. The narrator shows that the murder of Musa altered his own and his mother's lives for decades: his mother became obsessed with the death of her oldest son, and eventually Harun felt forced to exact a kind of vengeance by murdering a French Algerian.

Albert Camus *A Happy Death* (1936-1938, unpublished in Camus' lifetime)

In *A Happy Death*, Camus' first novel, the protagonist, Patrice Mersault, shares more than a surname with the Meursault of *The Stranger*: each is a shipping clerk working in Algiers, and each kills a man. An early Camus manuscripts bears as a subtitle "L'Etranger ou Un home heureux." Catherine Brosman comments that this wording, combining as it does the titles of the two later novels *La Mort heureuse* and *L'Etranger*, "show[s] not only the connection between the novels, which is integral, but also their common source in an earlier conception" (43). Many of the ideas explored in *The Stranger* are also evident in *A Happy Death*; indeed, the general consensus of critical opinion is that the earlier work was abandoned because Camus found in *The Stranger* a way of bringing together characters, settings, events and themes which remain disjointed and incoherent in *A Happy Death*.

The chronology (though not the literary structure) of both novels is essentially the same: the protagonist lives an inauthentic life in Algiers; he commits a murder; he thereby attains the potential for living (and dying) authentically. Patrice's life in Algiers is dominated by the eight hours of every day which he spends at the office and the sensual pleasure he pursues in his leisure. He is much more aware than is Meursault that the time he spends working takes away his freedom which indicates that from the start of the novel Patrice is much more consciously in "revolt" than is Meursault (*Happy* 41). In conversation with Patrice, the cripple Zagreus makes the point that "it takes time to be happy," and that it takes money to buy that time (*Happy* 43). The solution to Patrice's problem is to shoot Zagreus and take the considerable fortune which the crippled man had accumulated before the accident which left him paralyzed. Patrice is now free to pursue single-mindedly the happiness he has wanted all of his life.

The shooting of the crippled man raises the same moral problems as the shooting of the Arab; indeed, in his excellent Afterward, Jean Sarocchi refers to Patrice as taking advantage of Zagreus' trust in him to commit cold-blooded murder. This, however, ignores the fact that Zagreus is at the very least a willing co-conspirator in his own murder providing Patrice with the motive, the means and the opportunity. Zagreus wants Patrice to have the money to pursue what he calls Patrice's "'duty ... to live and be happy'" (*Happy* 38).

Although he now has the time to achieve a happy life, Patrice fails. He travels throughout Europe, returns to Algiers and lives for some time with three girls at the (aptly named) House Above the World, marries Lucienne, lives in isolation at a house in the Chenoua which overlooks the sea. (The exact relationship of these events is somewhat unclear.) It is only when he becomes terminally ill with heart failure brought on by pleurisy (ironically first evident a few hours after he kills Zagreus) that Patrice feels "he had at last attained what he was seeking ... [he] realized that his life and his fate were completed here and that henceforward all his efforts would be to submit to this happiness and to confront its terrible truth" (*Happy* 139-140). He understands that Lucienne will love another man once he is dead; he understands that authenticity of being cannot be measured in years; he has achieved the state of happiness. He dies with a smile because he does not fear death

Appendix 6: Bibliography

Works by Albert Camus

Camus, Albert. *A Happy Death*. Trans. Richard Howard. 1st Vintage International Edition. New York: Random House, 1995. Print.

---. *Caligula and Three Other Plays*. Trans. Stuart Gilbert. New York: Alfred A. Knopf, 1958. Print.

---. *Lyrical and Critical Essays*. 1968. Trans. Philip Thody. New York: Vintage Books, 1970. Print.

---. *Notebooks 1935-1942*. Trans. Philip Thody. New York: Alfred A. Knopf, 1963. Print.

---. *Notebooks 1942-1951*. Trans. Justin O'Brien. New York: Alfred A. Knopf, 1965. Print.

---. *Resistance, Rebellion, and Death*. Trans. Justin O'Brien. New York: Alfred A. Knopf, 1991. Print.

---. *The Fall*. Trans. Justin O'Brien. 1st Vintage International Edition. New York: Alfred A. Knopf, 1961. Print.

---. *The Myth of Sisyphus and Other Essays*. Trans. Justin O'Brien. 1st Vintage International Edition. New York: Random House, 1991. Print.

---. *The Rebel: An Essay on Man in Revolt*. Trans. Antony Bower. 1st Vintage International Ed. New York: Random House, 1991. Print.

---. *The Stranger*. Trans. Matthew Ward. 1st Vintage International Edition. New York: Random House, 1989. Print.

Biographies:

Brée, Germaine. *Albert Camus*. 1st ed. New York: Columbia University Press, 1964. Print.

Lottman, Herbert. *Albert Camus A Biography*. 1st ed. New York: Doubleday and Company, 1979. Print.

McCarthy, Patrick. *Camus*. 1st ed. New York: Random House, 1982. Print.

Todd, Olivier. *Albert Camus: A Life*. 1st ed. New York: Carroll & Graf Publishers, 1997. Print.

Zaretsky, Robert. *Albert Camus: Elements of a Life*. 1st ed. New York: USA: Cornell University Press, 2010. 1-160. Print.

Critical Works:

Akeroyd, Richard. *The Spiritual Quest of Albert Camus*. 1st ed. Tuscaloosa: Portals Press, 1976. Print.

Bloom, Harold, ed. *Albert Camus's The Stranger*. 1st ed. New York: Infobase Publishing, 2008. Print.

Bloom, Harold. *Novelists and Novels*. 1st ed. Philadelphia: Chelsea House, 2005. Print.

The Stranger by Albert Camus

Brosman, Catherine. *Literary Masters Volume 8 Albert Camus*. 1st ed. Detroit: The Gale Group, 2001. Print.
Brée, Germaine, ed. *Camus: A Collection of Critical Essays*. 1st ed. Englewood Cliffs: Prentice-Hall, 1962. Print.
Freeman, E. *The Theater of Albert Camus: A Critical Study*. 1st ed. London: Methuen Co. Ltd., 1971. Print.
Gay-Crosier, Raymond. *Literary Masterpieces Volume 8: The Stranger*. 1st ed. Detroit: The Gale Group, 2002. Print.
Hughes, Edward, ed. *The Cambridge Companion to Camus*. 1st ed. Cambridge: Cambridge University Press, 2007. Print.
Lazere, Donald. *The Unique Creation of Albert Camus*. 1st ed. New Haven: Yale U.P., 1973. Print.
Luppé, Robert de. *Albert Camus*. 1st ed. New York: Funk & Wagnalls, 1966. Print.
Maquet, Albert. *Albert Camus: The Invincible Summer*. 1st ed. New York: Humanities Press, 1972. Print.
Maus, Derek, ed. *Readings on The Stranger*. 1st ed. San Diego: Greenhaven Press, 2001. Print.
McCarthy, Patrick. *Camus The Stranger: A Student Guide*. 2nd ed. New York: Cambridge University Press, 2004. Print.
Parker, Emmett. *Albert Camus: The Artist in the Arena*. 1st ed. Madison and Milwaukee: University of Wisconsin, 1965. Print.
Petersen, Carol. *Albert Camus*. 1st ed. Trans. Alexander Gode. New York: Frederick Ungar Publishing, 1969. Print.
Rhein, Phillip. *Albert Camus*. 1st ed. Twayne Publishers, 1969. Print.
Sartre, Jean-Paul. "An Explication of *The Stranger*." Brée 108-121. Print.
Scherr, Arthur. "Camus's *The Stranger*." *Explicator* 59.3 Spring 2001: 149-53. Print.
Showalter Jr., English. *The Stranger Humanity and the Absurd*. 1st ed. Boston: Twayne Publishers, 1989. Print.
Sprintzen, David. *Camus: A Critical Examination*. Philadelphia: Temple University, 1988. Print.
Sprintzen, David, and Adrian van den Hoven. *Sartre and Camus: A Historical Confrontation*. 1st ed. Amherst: Humanity Books, 2004. Print.

Internet:
Bloom, Ryan. "Lost in Translation: What the First Line of 'The Stranger' Should Be." *New Yorker Online*. 15 May 2012: n. page. Web. 18 Jun. 2012.
Delahoyde, Michael. "Camus, *The Stranger*." *20th Century Arts & Humanities*. Washington State University, 2005. Web. 18 Jun 2012.
Edwards, Jonathan and Smolinski, Reiner, Editor. "Sinners in the Hands of an Angry God. A Sermon Preached at Enfield, July 8th, 1741." *Electronic Texts in*

American Studies. University of Nebraska - Lincoln, Web. 13 Sep.

Lee, Simon. "Albert Camus: Caligula Theatre of the Absurd." *Albert Camus Society.* 1 Jan. 2012. Web. 11 Nov. 2014.

Podhoretz, Norman. "Camus and His Critics: A Review of 'Camus' by Patrick McCarthy." *New Criterion.* 1 Nov. 1982. Web. 27 Nov 2014.

Simpson, David. "Albert Camus (1913 - 1960)." *The Internet Encyclopedia of Philosophy (IEP).* 2005. Web. 13 Jul 2012.

SparkNotes Editors. "SparkNote on *The Stranger.*" SparkNotes.com. SparkNotes LLC. 2003. Web. 8 Jun. 2012.

Stone, Kem. "Absurdist Camus - Caligula." *The Struggle of Sisyphus: Absurdity and Ethics in the Work of Albert Camus.* 1 July 2006. Web. 11 Nov. 2014.

The Stranger by Albert Camus

To the Reader

Ray strives to make his products the best that they can be. If you have any comments or questions about this book *please* contact the author through his email: **moore.ray1@yahoo.com**
Visit his website at **http://www.raymooreauthor.com**
Also by Ray Moore: Most books are available from amazon.com as paperbacks and at most online eBook retailers.

Fiction:
The Lyle Thorne Mysteries: each book features five tales from the Golden Age of Detection:
    Investigations of The Reverend Lyle Thorne
    Further Investigations of The Reverend Lyle Thorne
    Early Investigations of Lyle Thorne
    Sanditon Investigations of The Reverend Lyle Thorne
    Final Investigations of The Reverend Lyle Thorne

Non-fiction:
The Text and Critical Introduction series <u>differs</u> from the Critical introduction series as these books contain the original text and in the case of the medieval texts an interlinear translation to aid the understanding of the text. The commentary allows the reader to develop a deeper understanding of the text and themes within the text.
    "Sir Gawain and the Green Knight": *Text and Critical Introduction*
    "The General Prologue" by Geoffrey Chaucer: *Text and Critical Introduction*
    "The Wife of Bath's Prologue and Tale" by Geoffrey Chaucer: *Text and Critical Introduction*
    "Heart of Darkness" by Joseph Conrad: *Text and Critical Introduction*
    "The Sign of Four" by Sir Arthur Conan Doyle *Text and Critical Introduction*
    "A Room with a View" By E.M. Forster: *Text and Critical Introduction*
    "Oedipus Rex" by Sophocles: *Text and Critical Introduction*

The Critical Introduction series is written for high school teachers and students and for college undergraduates. Each volume gives an in-depth analysis of a key text:
    "The Stranger" by Albert Camus: A Critical Introduction (Revised Second Edition)
    "The General Prologue" by Geoffrey Chaucer: A Critical Introduction
    "Pride and Prejudice" by Jane Austen: A Critical Introduction

A Study Guide

"The Great Gatsby" by F. Scott Fitzgerald: A Critical Introduction

Study guides available in print- listed alphabetically by author
* denotes also available as an eBook
"ME and EARL and the Dying GIRL" by Jesse Andrews: A Study Guide
"Wuthering Heights" by Emily Brontë: A Study Guide *
"Jane Eyre" by Charlotte Brontë: A Study Guide *
"The Myth of Sisyphus" and "The Stranger" by Albert Camus: Two Study Guides *
"The Meursault Investigation" by Kamel Daoud: A Study Guide
"Great Expectations" by Charles Dickens: A Study Guide *
"The Sign of Four" by Sir Arthur Conan Doyle: A Study Guide *
"A Room with a View" by E. M. Forster: A Study Guide
"Looking for Alaska" by John Green: A Study Guide
"Paper Towns" by John Green: A Study Guide
"Unbroken" by Laura Hillenbrand: A Study Guide
"The Kite Runner" by Khaled Hosseini: A Study Guide
"A Thousand Splendid Suns" by Khaled Hosseini: A Study Guide
"Go Set a Watchman" by Harper Lee: A Study Guide
"On the Road" by Jack Keruoac: A Study Guide
"The Secret Life of Bees" by Sue Monk Kidd: A Study Guide
"An Inspector Calls" by J.B. Priestley: A Study Guide
"The Catcher in the Rye" by J.D. Salinger: A Study Guide
"Macbeth" by William Shakespeare: A Study Guide *
"Othello" by William Shakespeare: A Study Guide *
"Antigone" by Sophocles: A Study Guide *
"Oedipus Rex" by Sophocles: A Study Guide
"Cannery Row" by John Steinbeck: A Study Guide
"East of Eden" by John Steinbeck: A Study Guide
"Of Mice and Men" by John Steinbeck: A Study Guide *

Study Guides available as e-books:

"Heart of Darkness" by Joseph Conrad: A Study Guide
"The Mill on the Floss" by George Eliot: A Study Guide
"Lord of the Flies" by William Golding: A Study Guide
"Catch-22" by Joseph Heller: A Study Guide
"Life of Pi" by Yann Martel: A Study Guide
"Nineteen Eighty-Four by George Orwell: A Study Guide
"Selected Poems" by Sylvia Plath: A Study Guide
"Henry IV Part 2" by William Shakespeare: A Study Guide
"Julius Caesar" by William Shakespeare: A Study Guide
"The Pearl" by John Steinbeck: A Study Guide
"Slaughterhouse-Five" by Kurt Vonnegut: A Study Guide
"The Bridge of San Luis Rey" by Thornton Wilder: A Study Guide

Teacher resources: Ray also publishes many more study guides and other resources for classroom use on the 'Teachers Pay Teachers' website: http://www.teacherspayteachers.com/Store/Raymond-Moore

Printed in Great Britain
by Amazon